SILENT GLEAM

"Journey of Unveiling the Illusions of the Heart"

saloni yadav

A step closer to understanding the vast
spectrum of human emotions.

A LETTER TO ALL....

Dear Reader,

First and foremost, thank you for picking up this book. Your willingness to explore its pages mean the world to me. I wanted to take a moment to share with you the heart and soul behind "Silent Gleam: Journey of Unveiling the Illusions of the Heart" and how I hope it can be a companion on your own journey.
This collection of poems is born out of my own experiences with the complexities of emotions—those quiet moments that arrive unexpectedly, offering hope and light, even in the darkest times. The "silent gleam" represents these moments, illuminating the path forward when it feels like you are lost.
Through these poems, I hope to offer a mirror for your own heart's reflections, helping you to see and confront the illusions that often cloud our emotional landscapes. Whether it's the illusion of perfect love, the fear of loneliness, or the misplaced trust that we sometimes make. Remember, you are not alone in this journey. We all face moments of doubt, fear, and confusion, but it's in these moments that we can also find strength, hope, and clarity. It's a gentle reminder that every glimmer of light, no matter how small, can guide us through the darkest times.
As you read through these pages, I hope you find comfort in the words and reassurance that you are not alone. We are all in this together and finding solace in the shared understanding of our experiences.
Thank you for letting me be a part of your journey. May "Silent Gleam" be a source of light and hope for you, as it has been for me.

With warmth and gratitude,

Saloni

CONTENT

Journey begins...

CHAPTER 1

THE DUAL NATURE OF HOPE

saloni yadav

Hope is a trap.
All it does is,
make your desires snap.
As soon as you lower your guards,
and higher get your hopes,
the moment it slips down,
like a ball on the slope.

It's a word that,
the world is counting on.
A single thread keeping you up,
In the pool of miseries
From getting drowned.

saloni yadav

Hope,
For this single word,
A lot it takes,
Desires, soul, love interest,
All your life will be at stake.
Hoping is a holy word of gambling.
On its table, you're left on your own.
Only then you'll be the one surviving,
If fate plays the right pawn.

saloni yadav

It knows well about your weakness,
twisting your heart every second,
leaving you in the stage of bleakness,
making you utterly vulnerable,
impossible to keep your thoughts stable.

between the beginning and the end,
you get a lot to cope.
risking your heart and mind,
only path you see asks you to elope.

saloni yadav

But,
Hope's positivity shines,
a light through challenges and despair,
Guiding us forward, believing in better,
 even when life isn't fair.

 In every relation it is nurtured,
 hope promotes growth and light,
 Bringing hearts together,
 in the darkest night.

saloni yadav

hope with effort and faith always gets along.
in whichever relation it's invested,
only makes that bond strong.

hence,

this word is not always that wrong.

So let's cherish hope's power,
in every connection we find,
For it's hope that uplifts us,
and strengthens hearts and mind.

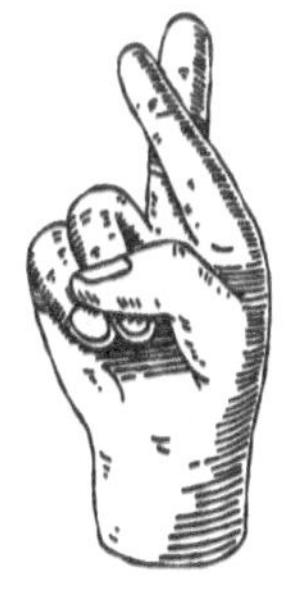

CHAPTER2

EVERLASTING FLAME

saloni yadav

To love, each heart has its own way,
yet warmth and longing light everyone's day.
passion's fire and desire's flame,
different paths, but all came to one end.

journeys rich with tales and dreams,
with trust and love, only the spirit beams.

saloni yadav

Stories shared, memories deep,
in these bonds, our hearts we keep.
what is the end, of this love's quest?
a mystery leaves us no rest.
for love's not a point to find,
but a journey, life entwined.

saloni yadav

In the little things we share,
Passion blooms beyond compare.
To keep love fresh, alive, anew,
Is a journey we pursue.

In every step, love's fire bright,
Together we conquer the night.
For love, a journey to forever be,
Keeping it fresh for eternity.

CHAPTER 3

BLOSSOMING ALONE
AND
TOGETHER

saloni yadav

She was fine being alone ,
Prepared to turn any upcoming stone,
on her own.

Enjoying her solitude,
Accepting all little, with gratitude.
Like this bunch of vines,
She blossomed just fine.
Every moment with time
She sways, leaps, thrives,
She realised.

saloni yadav

Running her finger over the stems, she mumbles,
'you seem enough',
'all ready ,to take any tough.'

until,
you get a support
expecting a few things you're gonna abort
you still blossom fine,
but it seems easier this time.

saloni yadav

there's someone to share
the weight beauty comes with
you now easily bear.
Growing alone seemed fine
but sharing a little
doesn't seem a bad sign.

and then,
after all together that you grew
leaving all the burden on you,
now it's time to remove that support,
before you knew.

saloni yadav

we were living,
that made us alive,
wish we could still live,
now that it's hard to survive.

CHAPTER 4

"CHASING THE GLEAM"

saloni yadav

The days you cried,
The days that haunt
Why do we remember them as,
"they weren't too harsh"
Why is the present so frustrating,
When it's the very thing
For which you've been waiting.

saloni yadav

There are some wishes
That you wished so much for,
Costing you your peace
and now scarring your heart.
Love, power, passion,
are only the beautiful journeys
mistaken for destinations,
in the name of possession.

saloni yadav

Happiness is like a mirage in the desert
Every single life is wishing for it,
Or is in the search.

When you think you've found one
And are ready to savor,
It slips through your fingers,
And moves a bit farther.

saloni yadav

As your grip on it tightens
It slips away like sand through the sieve
What you now live as a harsh present
Was once a beautiful wish to believe.

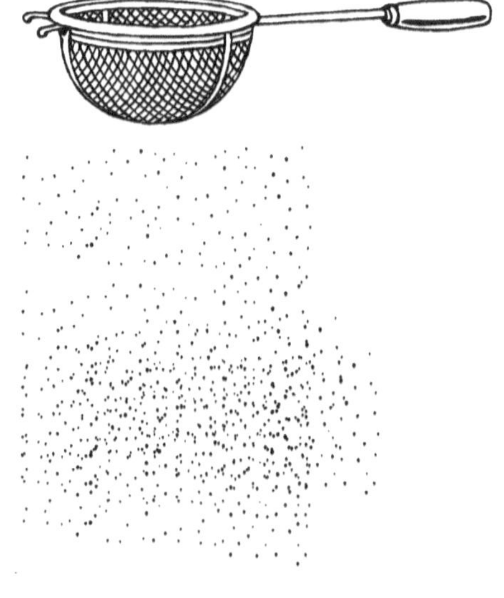

saloni yadav

Happiness is like a dandelion's spore,
Chased through fields, dancing in the breeze,
But as you catch it, it scatters evermore,
Leaving you to seek it again with ease.

Summing up all the cues and thoughts,
It's all the attraction to presentation,
 For you, there's a board of caution,
Happiness is a journey, not a destination.

saloni yadav

Happiness is elusive and delicate,
 like a whisper that can easily fade,
A fleeting moment in the sun,
where dreams and hopes are laid.

It dances just beyond our grasp,
a fleeting, shimmering gleam,
like a distant star that fades away,

yet still we chase the dream.

CHAPTER 5

WHISPERS OF LIBERATION

saloni yadav

In a room so dim, she gazes high,
A bird in the sky, freedom in its eye.
Wishing to be like ,that bird so free,
Escape the darkness, break society's decree.
Defy the norms , and be the real me.

Trapped in societal bounds, like a cage,
She envies the birds, which are free on life's stage.
Her inner voice whispers, "You too can fly ,
Break free from the chains, reach for the sky."

saloni yadav

"Yes," she replies, "but never as a bird,
I'll be a kite in the winds , unheard."
A kite in the gentle breeze, rises with delight,
symbolizing her joy,
only when she meets other's needs right.

In life's storms, she's blamed for being weak,
Harsh, judgmental words, the pain they speak.
Made to dance, controlled by a string,
A puppet in a play, where kindness could bring.
Her steps were light, yet her fate was tight
Bound by invisible threads, in a word devoid of light.

saloni yadav

All this time she was, controlled from afar,
Her struggles and strength, leaving a visible scar.
Letting winds of change, carry away her fear.
So she feels weightless, free, and sincere,

Yearning for freedom, lightness in her heart,
No blame on the kite, just a fresh start.

Breaking free from the ties that bind,
A journey to lightness, where true freedom finds

CHAPTER 6

SILENT ECHOES

saloni yadav

Deeper in hearts, where wishes lay,
I yearn for light, to guide my way.
mirror of my soul,
the eyes that show no tears,
Reflects the silent pain,
echoing through years.

saloni yadav

Against the wall, a burdened cry,
"I wish I could die these days,"
 echoes high.
As I lean to wail, it offers no embrace,
Pushing me away,
leaving my heart in its place.

Pressed to the pillow, silent cries,
Strangled whispers, darkness lies.

saloni yadav

Winds, having a tightening grasp,
Around my neck , a haunting clasp.
"I wish I could die these days,"
in shadows, slip.
Yearning for peace, where silence can eclipse.

saloni yadav

Starry hopes in a darkened sky
clouds swallow every gleam,
Darkness seeps through eyes,
 filling my heart's stream.

A wish to close my eyes, find the light within,
Guide me to sanity, a better place to begin.

saloni yadav

Wishing not for death in these despairing days,
Embracing the light within, where hope stays.
I wish I could die these days' fades away.
Hope's light emerges, guiding the way.

No more seeking other's light
Just to end this endless night.

CHAPTER 7

A SYMPHONY WITH MY PLANT

saloni yadav

In sync with my heart, the plant on my shelf,
Beating with its growth
whenever the sun shines itself.
Yet on gloomy days,
 when no gleam in sight,
Leaves curl in despair,
 mirroring my heart's tough fight
To conserve energy, branches bend low,
Like the plant, In solitude I also move slow.

saloni yadav

Rains of tears, a downpour of despair,
Roots soaked, branches heavy,
 it's all too much to bear.
n the soil of sorrow,
roots deeply weep,
With branches hanging low,
a sadness seeps.

Time crawls,
and I'm stuck in this rhyme,
Hoping for sunshine,
 in this rhythm of time

CHAPTER 8

DESPAIR TO HOPE

saloni yadav

She was lost in despair,
Every ounce of her, yet to be repaired.
Tired and weak,
packed the suitcase of her miseries
And was ready to leave.
The darkness in her path
Sank her heart.
But ,there lay a faith,
Beneath all the scars .

saloni yadav

And to her rescue–

Angels sent someone.
A shadow on the path.
Where once she walked alone,
Like winds to lighten her feet,
A presence to make her whole.

Someone like the Moon,
Who follows her everywhere,
Brightening the path
That now leads '*Somewhere*'.

saloni yadav

She smiled,
And whispered–

"you are Moon to me".
You brought back my hope,
With you, my heart no longer sore,
You are the moon I now adore."

CHAPTER 9

CYCLE OF EMOTION

saloni yadav

Right now I'm happy.
But more to it,
I'm afraid to have it.
It seems to fall out
Like sand in a fist.
I spent my happiness in fear,
Wasting every ounce of it.

saloni yadav

With fear in my heart,
I tighten the grip on it, hard.
Wishing for it to stay a bit longer
So, by the time it fades,
I would come out a little stronger.

saloni yadav

Holding on doesn't give any solution.
Enjoying it while it lasts is the only option.
Amid all those worries,
Do not lose the time's track.
The sole reason for happiness is to
keep every piece of you intact.

Because it's a cycle,
And it is gonna wheel back.

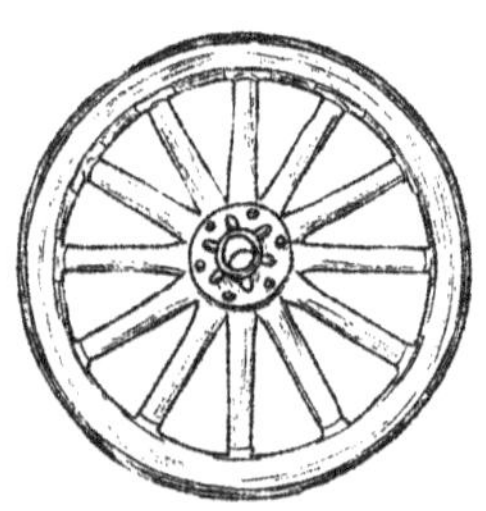

CHAPTER 10

PLEA TO THE NORTH STAR

saloni yadav

I'm sitting on my window,
It's monsoon, the sky's clear though.
The earthy scent of soil,
Tea on the stove boils.

Moon graces the starry nights,
Birds, weary from endless flights.

saloni yadav

I gaze at my north star,
It shines brighter as I start.

Oh dear,

How all these look serene and new,
From your shine to the morning's dew,
Living all their lives with grace, with truth.

saloni yadav

There's no place for me, it's clear.
The world of evil corrodes my shine,
Come rescue me,
Save me with your light, pure divine.
Please grant me this wish,
Let me find a life full of bliss.
Take me up there with you,
So that my inner light can truly bloom.

In your vast sky, alone,
I wish to shine with a light of my own

CHAPTER II

CHAINS OF SILENCE

saloni yadav

That moment in life
When everything feels uptight.
The soul weighs down,
Eyes all dried,
With no sign of tears.
Pain like a stake through the heart,
But not a single scream to hear.
Fingers on neck
As if being strangled to death.
Once in a lifetime, we've all faced this plight,
Where we want to cry, but hold back tight.
Unable to find a reason that justifies,
And that's the pain we try to disguise.

saloni yadav

In the silence, we carry the weight,
Invisible chains that bind our fate.
Hoping for a dawn to break,
A light to lift, a breath to take.

But in these quiet moments of despair,
We find a strength we didn't know was there.
A whispered hope, a soft, inner plea,
That one day soon, we'll be set free.

CHAPTER 12

CITY'S NOCTURNAL CHARM

saloni yadav

In the silent streets past midnight,
The city breathes, alive in its own right.
After hours of work, a gentle sigh,
As if the city's soul can finally fly.
The silence, a deep and soothing sound,
Converses with my soul, profound.
Tells me tales of its busy day,
In the stillness, our worries lay.

Night in village, their peace well-known,
Yet city nights have a charm of their own.
Amid the chaos of the day, unseen,
Little things add beauty, makes it serene.

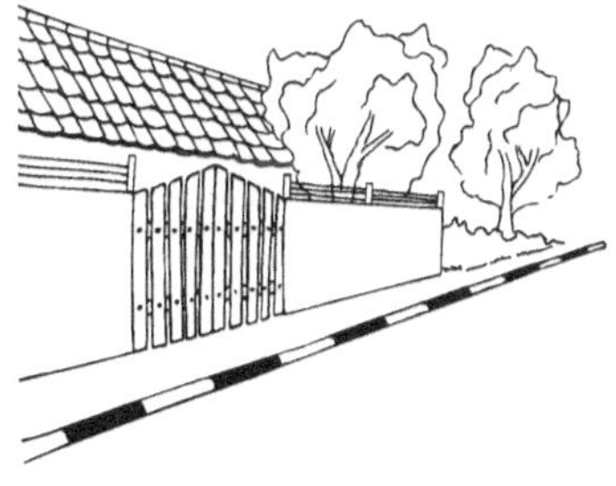

saloni yadav

As humans sleep, the city wakes,
In the stillness, a new rhythm takes
The moon, once hidden behind buildings,
Now shines above with silver beams,
Reflects on buildings, whispers dreams.

Stars once faint, now boldly gleam,
In the night, they fulfil their dream.

saloni yadav

Fireflies under moonlight's stream.
Dance in the median's green,
Glowing by the sidewalk, their light serene
Their flickering lights a hidden grace
Finding joy in their secret place.

saloni yadav

Man sits on the sidewalk's edge,
Plans his day, thoughts on a ledge.
Some talk to themselves only after twilight
Sorting out thoughts hidden from daylight.
Whispers lost in the still night air,
Moments of solitude, calm and rare.
A walk on these streets, once in a while,
Reveals the beauty missed by miles.

Paths we've walked for countless years
Now shimmer with echoes of forgotten tears

saloni yadav

Nostalgia lingers in the air,
a soft, tender smile,
Whispering memories of moments ,
gone by in style.
Each step we take brings memories to life,
In the quiet night, they soothe the restless mind.

saloni yadav

Beauty's near, in every glance,
In every shadow, in every chance.

Embrace the night, let the peace begin,
And feel the city's heart within.

CHAPTER 13

HOME WITHIN

saloni yadav

In search of shelter, I wandered all my life,
Walking on my toes, in search of light.
In hope of acceptance, to find a place to call,
Not every spot fits, but there is space for all.

In the downpour of despair
when your strength is frail,
Facing the world, feeling lost,
destined to fail.
Thought of birds in the rain,
wings flapping high,
Pause and dive deep,
to soar through the sky.

saloni yadav

You carry within you a hidden, silent scream,
Only heard when you're still,
like a whispered dream.
What you seek outside is already inside,
A place safe and warm, where you can confide.

I carry my home within, a sanctuary dear,
Where acceptance and understanding
are always near.
No matter where I wander,
comfort and strength I see,
In storms, I dive within,
as I carry my home with me.

saloni yadav

Rising above clouds, finding peace untold,
In this inner home, I am brave and bold.
True to myself, where I belong and always free,

My heart's true haven, I carry my home with me.

CHAPTER 14

CONFRONTING PAIN

saloni yadav

In the stillness of my tears, where feelings align,
 No matter the intensity, this ache is mine.
Others may laugh, call it exaggeration,
But I know my truth, my inner sensation.

Invisible to some, this internal fight,
Yet it's real, affecting my beautiful life.
Ignore the doubters, their disbelief never matter,
For me, it's a pain if it hurts.

saloni yadav

Listen closely to the whispers within,
Acknowledge the hurt, where it begins.
No shame in admitting, seeking remedy's course,
To heal from within, find a calming force.

Each ache and throb, a message to heed,
Not just in body, but where spirit's freed.
Take care of yourself, as your spirit flirts,
For truly, it's a pain if it hurts.

saloni yadav

Embrace the journey, through peaks and falls,
Finding strength within these hallowed walls.
Others may dismiss, their words stung,
Yet for me, it's a pain if it hurts.

 Unseen wounds are deeper, than they appear,
Invisible struggles, yet so crystal clear.
No need to compare, each journey asserts,
That for each of us, it's a pain if it hurts.

You have you……

and that's enough.